Ecuador

& the Galápagos Islands

Rob Rachowiecki

LONELY PLANET PUBLICATIONS
Melbourne • Oakland • London • Paris

ECUADOR

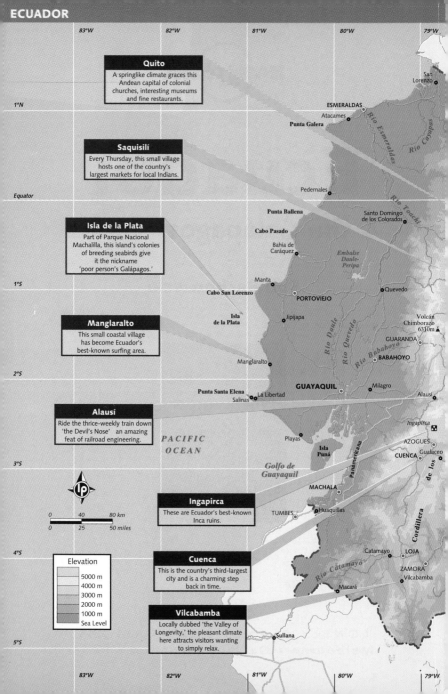

Quito
A springlike climate graces this Andean capital of colonial churches, interesting museums and fine restaurants.

Saquisilí
Every Thursday, this small village hosts one of the country's largest markets for local Indians.

Isla de la Plata
Part of Parque Nacional Machalilla, this island's colonies of breeding seabirds give it the nickname 'poor person's Galápagos.'

Manglaralto
This small coastal village has become Ecuador's best-known surfing area.

Alausí
Ride the thrice-weekly train down 'the Devil's Nose' — an amazing feat of railroad engineering.

Ingapirca
These are Ecuador's best-known Inca ruins.

Cuenca
This is the country's third-largest city and is a charming step back in time.

Vilcabamba
Locally dubbed 'the Valley of Longevity,' the pleasant climate here attracts visitors wanting to simply relax.

Elevation
5000 m
4000 m
3000 m
2000 m
1000 m
Sea Level

0   40   80 km
0   25   50 miles

1°N
Equator
1°S
2°S
3°S
4°S
5°S

83°W   82°W   81°W   80°W   79°W

San Lorenzo
ESMERALDAS
Atacames
Punta Galera
Río Esmeraldas
Río Cayapas
Río Teaone
Pedernales
Punta Ballena
Santo Domingo de los Colorados
Cabo Pasado
Bahía de Caráquez
Embalse Daule Peripa
Manta
Quevedo
Cabo San Lorenzo
PORTOVIEJO
Isla de la Plata
Jipijapa
Volcán Chimborazo 6310m ▲
GUARANDA
Río Daule
Río Quevedo
Río Babahoyo
BABAHOYO
Manglaralto
GUAYAQUIL
Milagro
Alausí
Punta Santa Elena
La Libertad
Salinas
Ingapirca
Playas
Isla Puná
AZOGUES
Gualaceo
CUENCA
Cordillera de los
PACIFIC OCEAN
Golfo de Guayaquil
MACHALA
Huaquillas
TUMBES
Catamayo
LOJA
Cordillera
ZAMORA
Vilcabamba
Río Catamayo
Macará
Sullana
Panamericana

2   Contents

ECUADOR

Otavalo
Ecuador's most famous Indian-crafts market boasts bargains galore!

Flotel Orellana
This floating hotel staffed by naturalist guides gives visitors a comfortable look at Río Aguarico.

Jungle Lodges
Rustic but comfortable jungle hotels on Río Napo and other rivers offer guided wildlife-watching opportunities.

Parque Nacional Cotopaxi
The Andean scenery here is dominated by the cone-shaped Volcán Cotopaxi (5897m).

Tena
Not only a good base for jungle trips, Tena is fast becoming the nation's premier kayaking and river-rafting destination.

Galápagos Islands
The legendary fearlessness of the wildlife makes these islands a must for naturalists who can afford the trip.

Ecuador & the Galápagos Islands
5th edition – February 2001
First published – February 1986

Published by
Lonely Planet Publications Pty Ltd ABN 36 005 607 983
90 Maribyrnong St, Footscray, Victoria 3011, Australia

Lonely Planet Offices
Australia Locked Bag 1, Footscray, Victoria 3011
USA 150 Linden St, Oakland, CA 94607
UK 10a Spring Place, London NW5 3BH
France 1 rue du Dahomey, 75011 Paris

Photographs
All of the images in this guide are available for licensing from
Lonely Planet Images.
W www.lonelyplanetimages.com

Front cover photograph
Conolophus subcristatus on South Plaza Island, the Galápagos
Islands (Tom Ulrich/Tony Stone Images)

Title page photograph
Galápagos Wildlife Guide (Sally Dillon)

ISBN 0 86442 761 1

text & maps © Lonely Planet Publications Pty Ltd 2001
photos © photographers as indicated 2001

Printed by SNP SPrint (M) Sdn Bhd
Printed in Malaysia

Although the authors and Lonely Planet try to make the information as accurate as possible, we accept no responsibility for any loss, injury or inconvenience sustained by anyone using this book.

Contents

THE WESTERN LOWLANDS 341

THE NORTH COAST 359

THE SOUTH COAST 399

THE GALÁPAGOS ISLANDS 436

4   Contents

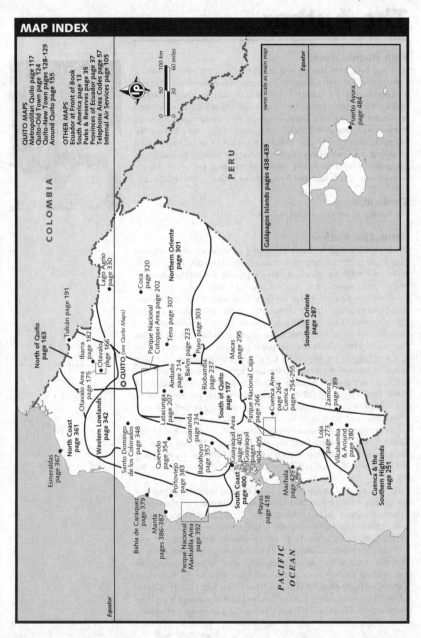

MAP INDEX

QUITO MAPS
Metropolitan Quito page 117
Quito-Old Town page 124
Quito-New Town pages 128–129
Around Quito page 155

OTHER MAPS
Ecuador at Front of Book
South America page 13
Parks & Reserves page 35
Provinces of Ecuador page 37
Telephone Area Codes page 57
Internal Air Services page 105

100 km
50
60 miles
30
0

COLOMBIA

PERU

Equator

same scale as main map

Galápagos Islands pages 438–439

Puerto Ayora
page 484

Tulcán page 191

Lago Agrio
page 330

Coca
page 320

North of Quito
page 163

Ibarra
page 182

Otavalo
page 166

Otavalo Area
page 175

QUITO (see Quito Maps)

Parque Nacional
Cotopaxi Area page 202

Northern Oriente
page 301

Tena page 307

Puyo page 303

Baños page 223

Macas
page 295

Ambato
page 214

Latacunga
page 207

Southern Oriente
page 287

Western Lowlands
page 342

Riobamba
page 237

Guaranda
page 234

Parque Nacional Cajas

Cuenca Area
page 264

Cuenca
pages 254–255

Santo Domingo
de los Colorados
page 348

Quevedo
page 354

Babahoyo
page 357

Zamora
page 289

Guayaquil Area
page 403

Guayaquil
pages
404–405

Loja
page 273

North Coast
page 361

Portoviejo
page 383

Esmeraldas
page 367

Vilcabamba
& Around
page 280

Cuenca & the
Southern Highlands
page 251

South Coast
page 400

Bahía de Caráquez
page 379

Manta
pages 386–387

Machala
page 428

Parque Nacional
Machalilla Area
page 392

Playas
page 418

PACIFIC
OCEAN

South of Quito
page 197

Equator

The Author

Rob Rachowiecki

Rob was born near London and became an avid traveler while still a teenager. He has visited countries as diverse as Greenland and Thailand. He spent most of the 1980s in Latin America – traveling, mountaineering and teaching English – and he now works in Peru and Ecuador part time as a leader for Wilderness Travel, an adventure-travel company. He is also the author of three other Lonely Planet guides – *Peru*, *Costa Rica* and the US guide *Southwest* – and he has contributed to LP's *South America on a shoestring* and *Central America on a shoestring*. In addition, he has worked on books by other publishers. When not traveling, he lives in Arizona with his wife, Cathy, and their three children – Julia, Alison and David.

Dedication

For JulsBaguls, because she is a real jewel!

From the Author

Three separate trips to Ecuador followed by innumerable emails and phone calls made this completely updated edition possible. Many people in Ecuador made my visits both more enjoyable and satisfyingly informative, and I would like to especially thank the following.

As always, the great staff at the Quito clubhouse of the South American Explorers set me straight on numerous issues. Jane Letham, a former South American Explorers manager, provided me with a seemingly inexhaustible stream of comments about anything to do with Quito. My friend Nancy Pelaez of Hostal Villa Nancy provided support, information and hospitality far and beyond the call of duty. Jean Brown of Safari Tours provided detailed information on the Galápagos and drove me around a dizzying number of lodges south of Quito and in the Mindo area, all the while dropping lovely tidbits of information from her encyclopedic knowledge of Ecuador. In Mindo, Tom Quesenberry helped with local information and followed up with several emails.

Steve Nomchong of Yacu Amu Rafting and Gynner Coronel of Ríos Ecuador are without any doubt the most knowledgeable river runners in Ecuador, and I greatly appreciate the time they both spent in educating me in the ways that river rafting and kayaking are growing rapidly in the country.

In the Oriente, Douglas McMeekin of Yachana Lodge invited me to a memorable Amazon-style Thanksgiving lunch and was a great source of information about the area. Arnaldo Rodriguez of Canodros provided me with scads of information about the Achuar people and the Kapawi Ecolodge. Kathy Kiefer kindly shared her knowledge of the Papallacta area with me. The Honorable Mayor of Zamora cordially mailed me a map of that town because the map was unavailable when I visited. I also enjoyed eye-opening conversations about the region with Randy Borman of Zabalo, geologist Mark Thurber, Lee Schel of the Sacha Lodge, director of the Eloy Alfaro Military College Coronel Luis B Hernández P, Santiago Herrera of Rain Forestur and Randy Smith of Coca – among many others.

In Otavalo, anthropologist Rodrigo Mora provided much information about the area. South of Quito, the delightful and charming Mignon Plaza told great stories at the Hacienda San Agustín de Callo. Owen Stevens accompanied me on hikes in Cotopaxi. Tom Walsh of Riobamba gave me a fantastic inside look at the lives of the *campesinos* in remote parts of Chimborazo Province. Eduardo Quito of Cuenca taught me much about that area, including Parque Nacional Cajas. In Vilcabamba, Orlando & Alicia Falco of the Rumi-Wilco Ecolodge were a great source of maps and information, especially about Parque Nacional Podocarpus, as was the friendly manager of the Hidden Garden. I also thank Avetur staff for a tour of many of the hotels in and around Vilcabamba.

On the coast, my thanks go to Jacob Santos, Daniel Proaño and Nicola Mears (all of Bahía de Caráquez), who gave me much insight into their local area. Director Eric Hortman personally guided me around the Bosque Protector Cerro Blanco. Peace Corps volunteer Rick Rhodes introduced me to the new Museo de Amantes de Sumpa, in the Santa Elena Peninsula. Helpful conversations with Clarisse Stong of Pro-Pueblo, Francisco Frias of Montañita, the folks at Tres Palmeras restaurant, ornithologist Nancy Hilgut and a host of others helped me pull this section together.

Have I forgotten somebody? I'm sure I have, and I apologize. To everyone who sent me reports and helped me gather information, a hearty 'Mil gracias!!' Folks who wrote in are acknowledged at the end of the book.

Finally, I hug my dear and wonderful children – chess player and pianist Julia, soccer player Alison and Lego player David – for understanding that Dad has to work in Ecuador for weeks on end; and my wife, Cathy, for keeping things on an even keel while I'm on the road. Thank you all.

Readers can contact me with comments, criticisms or updates at robrachow@earthlink.net, but I regret that I am unable to plan your trip for you! I do acknowledge all emails.

This Book

FROM THE PUBLISHER

The 5th edition of *Ecuador & the Galápagos Islands* was edited by Wendy Taylor, under the enlightened guidance of senior editor Maria Donohoe and with the assistance of Amelia Borofsky, Susan Derby, Paul Sheridan, Vivek Wagle, and Suki Gear. The maps were created by workhorse Sean Brandt, under the direction of the ever vigilant senior cartographer Monica Lepe. Matt DeMartini helped Sean by drawing some maps, and Kat Smith and Chris Gillis helped edit a few maps. Ken DellaPenta indexed the book.

The colorwraps were designed by Jennifer Steffey. In addition to taming the wildlife guide and creating the cover, Wendy Yanagihara designed the book, with the help of Margaret Livingston and Joshua Schefers and under the leadership of design manager Susan Rimerman. Beca Lafore coordinated the illustrations, and Justin Marler and Alan Tarbell drew exciting new ones. Other illustrations were the work of Mark Butler, Hugh D'Andrade, John Fadeff, Hayden Foell, Beth Grundvig, Lara Sox Harrison, Pablo Sanaguano, Jim Swanson and Hannah Reineck.